AF254729

ALMOST A MEMOIR

ALMOST A MEMOIR

POEMS BY

M.C. RYDEL

atmosphere press

© 2022 M.C. Rydel

Published by Atmosphere Press

Cover design by Senhor Toca
Cover Photograph by Stephanie Ross

No part of this book may be reproduced without permission from the author except in brief quotations and in reviews.

atmospherepress.com

For my sister, Christine

CONTENTS

CHAPTER ONE

MONTHS OF IMMORTALITY

Everyone in my family
Dies during the month of October.
You've got to know that about us
Before you get involved.
My grandfather died a lieutenant
In the Battle of Argonne Forest
About a month before the Armistice.
He left two little children behind.
My dad, the younger one,
Lived almost to the year 2000.
He walked in red and yellow woods
Every October day till the very end.
We found him on a park bench
The wind flapping his trench coat lapels.

My sister's the bravest of us all.
She skydives every autumn weekend,
Finds midweek deals in Colorado
To ski the expert runs;
Been known to jump out of taxicabs
Right in the worst part of the city
And gets drunk in costume on Halloween night,
Screaming about immortality, like a god.
Everyone in my family
Dies during the month of October.
You've got to know that about us
Before you get involved.

Indestructible. I am indestructible.
The next eleven months are mine.
I can manipulate time zones with an *app*.
My nieces and nephews, daughters and sons,
Don't look before jaywalking.
My dogs run through open gates.
My cats safely cross the busiest streets.
Yet the people who haven't met me yet
Don't know a thing about my fate.

I am the master of my existence,
The shaper of unshaped destiny.
I am immortal until the light of the next October sun
Makes me dance until the long, long month is done.

FIVE MINUTES WITH BRODSKY

He was used to getting many gifts:
American cigarettes, blue jeans,
Bottles of Johnnie Walker,
Smuggled letters and manuscripts,
Women with long dark hair,
His Soviet ID card stamped "Jew"
And from God – the poetry –
Every trope and scheme,
Every word bled from God's brow
And dripped from his apartment ceiling
Making brown water marks and blurring
The blue Cyrillic ink in his notebook.

Three hundred seconds on a New Year's Eve
That's what I got – a wooden door on a village street –
The foyer – a view of his single room.
The gifts? Two books added to his dozens.
He was a torn shirt and twenty accented words:
"I am shit today. My heart. I am more or less terrible.
Come back some other time. We will talk."
Thirty years later, I watch pedestrians on Morton Street
Walk from the Hudson River to Washington Square,
Unaware that I have them on a satellite view on my computer.

I practice the necromancy of desire,
Burn hair in the flame of a black candle,
Hear snatches of conversation beyond the shroud.
They sound like a confusing welter of howls
And hollow sounds that make you briefly go mad.
Brodsky holds in his hand the melted wax of a green candle
Molded into a half-inch square.
His body is highlighted in Shadowland with a sickly,
Glowing, green-white aura until he disappears,
And all that remains are his words, which is really all
That could ever remain, words spoken father to son,
Father to daughter, words on a page like a gift.

TO NATHAN AT HOME READING PABLO NERUDA

The past and future are crowded with reflections
And projections, sundresses with bare shoulders,
Moving boxes taped shut, unmarked, silent;
The present exists like a hollow reed.
Its music waits like air in a set of lungs.
It is an empty house waiting for foreclosure
As birds outside sing, a refrigerator hums,
A furnace exhales, a few scraps of paper
Peer out of the old shag carpet like mice.
The past clinks like brown beer bottles and sizzles
Like a grill full of steaks; the future is a fishing line
Taut in a still, waveless, glassy lake.

Meanwhile, Nathan's at home reading Pablo Neruda.
His life is a mountain river rife with rapids.
He's as tall and strong and angular as a Roman soldier,
As quiet as a guitar erect on its stand,
As old as a soul halfway to Nirvana,
As young as the new snow he melts in his hands.
Today, in conversation, he'll reference the decades
Lived before he was conceived; his waitress
Will chew her gum in wonder and just stare.
He will think of this – an old man's ghost in a young man's shape,
And he will compare the philosophies of Heaven and Hell,
As he drinks black coffee and writes his first villanelle.

VILLANELLE FOR THOSE WITHOUT A CARE

I don't have to be anywhere.
Whistles and time clocks don't mean anything
Anymore; I haven't a single care.

I conjure up an infinite number of rare
Places not to be, and I can sing:
"I don't have to be anywhere."

I float on a raft beneath bridges where
Siren-soaked, weary-eared crowds don't dream
Anymore; I haven't a single care.

I toss pinecones on a fire and stare
At midday clouds that all of a sudden mean
I don't have to be anywhere.

See, when sunsets sink and streetlamps glare
And phantoms fail to rise from their steam
Anymore; I haven't a single care.

My dreams are things of never and nowhere
Like the melted wax and feathers of a sunburnt wing
I don't have to be anywhere
Anymore; I haven't a single care.

SUICIDE MOTHS

The moths fly near this deserted
Stretch of county line road
     Just waiting for the right car to pass.

They find your windshield with style
     Just ahead of the dragonflies in the grill.

How many other suicides have you known?
Train track jumpers, sleeping pillers,
     Politicians found dead in the river,

Suicide bombers dying for a cause,
Suicide girls in video chat rooms.
     But none of them die like the suicide moths.

Their little souls pass right into you,
Entering your chest as you drive
     Joining your soul as it forever renews.

EDDIE AT THE DOOR

The man had soldier hands that knew
Each tooth of his house keys
At one or two A.M.

And traced the inhuman path
Of circuit boards
The next day,
Like a professor teaching
Hieroglyphics in braille.

Now, Eddie's whole job
Is a diamond-shaped chip
So thin it is hard to pick up.

Eddie would submerge his hands
In dishwater all the time
And turn every part red,

Except for the long thumbnail
He would use to chip food
Off the good china.

See, Eddie is at the door, now.
He is clutching your hands
With his old, red, scalded ones

As I make a paper airplane,
A task for years I couldn't do
Out of the first draft of this elegy
That for years
I just couldn't write.

AN ELEGY TO UNCLE RAY

I never thought I'd talk to your gravestone

     When I was a little boy
     Who would talk to imaginary people
     When you weren't looking.

But here we are among scarlet leaves
     With yellow ones still on the trees,

And I think we should have buried you
alongside your car,
     With a transistor radio,
     So you could change the oil
     To the sound of the ballgame.

Maybe we could have brought you back
Little by little through me
When I work all Saturday
     Soiling the fingernails
     I've finally begun to stop biting.

Maybe I'd awaken to the murmurs
Of a boy sleeping on my couch all night
     Or turn around when I scramble eggs
     To see him study his face in the toaster.

I think all I want now is to let you live
In a glance or a yawn or a nod
     When we take a ride in my car after church
     With nowhere particular we need to go.

LETTER TO ANTIGONE

You died so young the dates
Were never chiseled into your gravestone –
Immortality through neglect.

See, in tragedy, everything is clean,
Flawless, inevitable, hopeless, and known.
All are bound to their parts.

You buried a brother with a handful of soil
Then died a scripted destiny
Like a future performance of your play.

What gods keep you company in the afterlife?
Why is your heaven
Alive only in the dreams of the living?

Where feet get caught in a quicksand blanket,
Where gardens suddenly materialize,
Where a fly crawls on their shoulders

Like an uninvited update to a cell phone
From some satellite spinning overhead,
Or like a box of war coins found hidden in a closet:

Swastikas, Lira, Francs, and Shillings.
You find life in memories and serendipity
And make yourself known to us by hiding sets of keys.

Tell me you still leave ingredients out of the recipes
You share with other phantoms. Tell me you still dabble
With myths and magic. Find something bad to say about someone,

And come back to the living through some dreamer's mirror,
When your dark eyes, bright and sly,
Burn themselves into the dreamer's reflection

And make her cringe, and make her run,
Make her move with tremendous speed over vast distances,
Chased by someone she never even knew.

You died so young the dates
Were never chiseled into your gravestone —
Achieving immortality through neglect.

LOST DREAMS

If you want to forget a nightmare,
Open a window and stare outside,
So a Slavic mother's folklore goes.

Every unbearable dream burns off
Like yellow swirling fog into oblivion.

Even the repeating ones are forgotten
As the April dreams in June
That you exaggerate for a therapist.

All of my dreams get lost
In a place where we are the dreams
And the bizarre commonplace.

Where nightmares,
Are the paths you take
To gain admission into real dreamland.

Where flowers reach for sunshine in moonlight,
Dogs catch squirrels, cats lose mice,
Ulysses and Penelope bicker for twenty years,

Angels compare the planets
And civilizations they've changed,

And alchemists turn pearly oyster shells
Into necklaces of stones that glow.

I have lost all of my dreams.
I'll need a police report to file a claim
The insurance company will decline.

In the end, the sleep I need to keep
Will seem as real as the scent of toast,

The taste of a morning cigarette,
Poodles moving room to room in a pack,
And the handle of the boiling pot vibrating
As eggshells bob up and down
Till my medicine kicks in.

16

DAUGHTERS OF TIME

My family visits me when they can.
The days, so few remaining, pass quietly;
Orderlies, nurses, doctors, and nuns
Talk in the hall as if we weren't even here.

I'm counting on an amazing recovery,
Unhook the monitors, cease the morphine drip,
Eject the catheter, and join the endless procession
Of days in Jamaica en route to oblivion.

My family would be happier too.
A daughter and a son in love with spouses in Ocho Rios.
A wife and sister reading at the pool.
A brother-in-law wearing a wide-brimmed hat.

Each dancing dervish diadem speckled
Day's the vacation you've always sought.
Stars and a full moon, pitchers of rum hurricanes,
A grill, reggae, herbs, and fantasies.

I declare the mornings as mine
As everyone sleeps, the Caribbean breeze,
The Jamaican coffee, I pen a pantoum
At daybreak in a cool breakfast room.

My daughter's the first one up.
Her beauty. Her grace. Her eyes.
Like a woman Ulysses, she's become a name,
A scepter, an island, and future fame.

She says she's off for a run
From hotel to cathedral to tower.
The sun rises above the blue sea.
My lovely wife makes a pot of tea.

My family visits me when they can.
The days, so few remaining, pass quietly;
Orderlies, nurses, doctors, and nuns
Talk in the hall as if we weren't even here.

PANTOUM CHANNELING A VOODOO QUEEN

We should have suspected the half-price seat
At an outdoor séance, the self-inflicted evil eyes,
Chakra cleansing, realignment, tarot and palm
And Suprina turning into a voodoo queen.

Yet, an outdoor séance, the self-inflicted evil eyes,
Makes an appealing evening in New Orleans,
And Suprina turning into a voodoo queen
Invokes melancholy, reverence, and the sublime.

See, an appealing Spring evening in New Orleans,
Like a spirit breeze far from the Quarter
Invokes melancholy, reverence, and the sublime
As light as rising cigarette smoke,

And like a spirit breeze far from the Quarter,
Suprina gets under our skin like innuendo
As light as rising cigarette smoke
And as heavy as a waterfall of luggage.

Suprina gets under our skin like innuendo,
Like a prophet implying there's no life or death;
And as heavy as a waterfall of luggage.
Her head tumbles and rolls to our feet.

Like a prophet implying there's no life or death,
She exhales the history of her people in her last breath.
Her head tumbles and rolls to our feet
And we should have suspected the half-price seat.

THE DAY WE LEARNED TO READ PALMS

For Mary Ann

I took an afternoon nap
And dreamt we fled to high ground.
We let the river have the house
And found a clearing in the hills,
Where we could see
Newspaper boxes floating in town
Around the telephone booth,
Where some dog was perched
Howling for its master,
Who was hiding somewhere
In these hills.

Your cooking woke me, though.
I looked out the bedroom window
And nearly forgot the dream.
Some kids from the ridge,
Wading in our creek,
Had thrown their clothes
On the trunk and hood
Of my car.
I stopped myself
From screaming at them
And lay on my back.

All I could hear was wind chimes,
You singing as you cooked,
And some crickets
Chirping in the reeds,
When I looked at my hands again.
What have we seen here today?
A lifeline to the wrist,
Twins parallel to the fingers?
Lines on something

That could lose all feeling
If I lay my head on it too long.
I should have gone downstairs
Help you make the salad,
Stop halfway through
And touch you on both shoulders.
You'd put a spoon in my mouth
And laugh as you walk away.
Instead I stayed upstairs
Until you called me,
Knowing we saw what we wanted
In our palms earlier that day.

AUTUMN

We all think of leaves,
Hectic red and yellow shells
Clattering on cobblestones,
Waking us up early
Like a coach in morning mist.

We make Sunday breakfast,
Imagine ourselves innkeepers,
Decorate lintels with gourds
And distill this year's harvest
Into warm cider for our guests.

You take a couple for a walk
On our land, point out the hands
Asleep among the bales.

I let others get blisters raking
While I bake squash for dinner
And consider the shadow of leaves
Spread across the kitchen floor,
And think of phantoms
Instead of the west wind
Sifting through your fine hair
When you walk home alone.

And we end up making ourselves
Miserable in moonlight
Supposed to calm our frantic minds
The way an early frost quiets the woods.

In the morning you leave me
Among our plaid, well-fed guests
Who see loose clouds torn above
And think of them as leaves.

ECLIPSE

I race a snowstorm home,
Watch the broken clouds
Drift past the winter moon
Above every stoplight,
Feel its beams spook others
Into running the red lights,
And worry whether I will get
To see the eclipse tonight.

But I am really racing to you,
Or something I think of
That's supposed to be you:
A black and white film clip
Of a woman writing
A letter in the light
Of the evening news
And wondering if I crashed
Every time the cell phone vibrates.

Some of our neighbors
Stand on their lawns;
The tripods of their telescopes
Ankle deep in the snow,
Their breath in the cold air
Rises to the shrinking moon
Like a ghost at the second coming
When I finally arrive home.

That's when I go up
To the attic to clear a spot
Beneath the skylight,
Look through the Venetian blinds
Off to the side,
And see our best friends
Next door in their kitchen below
Drinking coffee, talking slowly

About something I'll never know.
At last, you join me.
Thin clouds pass in moonlight.
Soon the snow over the suburbs
Will get here and fall on our gabled roof,
But for now we'll just lie here
And feel amazed by the shadow
That we are just a little part of
Eclipse the winter moon.

A TUSCAN EPITHALAMION

For Stephanie and Bryant

We've traveled thousands of miles to get here,
Where it all began for the two of you

In Italy, in Tuscany, in Lucignano.
This village of old walls, sunsets, and love.

You have journeyed far already.
Canoed down a mountain stream

Rode camels in the desert near Fez
And galloped horseback on Spanish plains.

You've rented a helicopter. Flipped a canoe.
Sailed a Great Lake, maneuvered a sports car.

Got drunk on a bus and fell asleep on a train.
And you've been together only five years.

In this country of Phoebus and Bacchus,
In this land of vineyards and sun,

Call forth the muses. Let the words echo.
Watch the constellations shift every night.

As Perseus rescues Andromeda in the northern sky
Where space grows infinite with time,

You'll start a new journey, your eternal return,
Austria, Lichtenstein, and Prague.

Amor fati. Love the good and the bad.
Your lives entwined forever again and again.

Sleep without worries. Dream of the future.
Take full advantage of this quiet night.

TO MY SISTER

In Polish, our name means spade.
It's a gravedigger's shovel,
A sharpened blade
Wielded first
By some round, brown hood
Burying peasants.

He gets blisters from our name.
Wears it out till its middle
Looks like the window
On a gliding planchette
Stopping over the letters
On Ouija board coffins.

But souls don't rise to the glass
As he works in the chill of the Polish sun,
And the souls don't spell out the names
Of unborn uncles and cousins
Conceived by vergers and sextons
Who buried themselves in their wives.

No. Our gravedigger held onto the spade
Until he sold it at the market
And changed his name and trade.

And now my sister,
What shall it be?
Let's sit on a tombstone
In a full moon

And toss a coin to see
Which one of us
Will trudge from the cemetery
And talk with an accent
We've learned watching B-movies.

PLACEBO EFFECT

My sister's been part of a clinical study
For a couple of weeks now.
Blue pills every four hours:
Six, ten, and two to start the day;
Six and ten at night before bed.

There's no way really of knowing
If the cure's made from a flower from Peru
Or just sugar pills (snap, crackle, pop)
Plain or peanut, amazingly effective
On the symptoms, but incriminatingly sweet.

Last night, she threw her glasses into the river,
Tight-rope, balance beamed a bridge,
Recognized each boat by the sound of its motor
Differentiated the cargo by its scent
As the wind shifts from gale to zephyr.

The 6 am dose helps her walk the dogs.
The 10 am has a cocaine rush.
The 2 pm is 2:30 tomorrow morning in Mumbai.
The 6 pm dose suppresses all appetites.
And the 10 pm shows as glucose in a blood panel.

She hopes this is all just the placebo effect,
Fooling herself and her body into immortality,
Wondering if she's swallowing a lie
Or taking a dose at 2 am of the real thing, the real thing,
The only subject in the study to live, and to live to sing.

MY LEBANESE FRIEND

Everyone should have one.
A friend who values honesty,
Promises, vows, bonds, and oaths
Above all else – point, counterpoint.
A friend who says things you don't
Want to hear, alienates your other friends,
Gets detained at Customs
Even though he's American.

He is used to talking himself out of trouble.
Like an ancient Phoenician explorer,
Willing to assimilate but changing everything
Just by the way his accent sounds.
He has learned to control his temper.
He speaks English like a librarian.
Truth replaces beauty and everyone knows
Exactly how everyone else feels.

Spending time with him passes like the end
Of a long vacation, when you decide
To put your house keys back in your pocket,
Take that last morning walk on the beach,
Screw around with the resort's street signs,
Bump every bumper unparking,
And leave your Lebanese friend behind to tell the truth
Like a novelist daily perfecting his prose to tell a lie.

BAT HUNTING

Whenever we kids know they're near,
Somebody finds a wool sweater
Soaks it in water
And throws it straight up.

It must be the sound
Flapping sleeves make
That attracts them.

Every toss, faint waves,
The kind that skydivers hear
Playing in the strings
Of their parachutes,
Brings them a little closer.

And we think the way they do,

Knowing nothing other
Than the flight of that sweater.

Watching every motion
From the back billowing
In the damp dusk air
To the water drawings
The torso leaves
When it lands.

Not until we are bats ourselves
Do they arrive;

From courtyards and attics
A dozen of them
Converge on the sweater,

Then on us,
Until we've got bats
Dipping among our shoulders.

We trap them
In our fingers,
Bring them close enough
To feel our shallow breath,
Then, just let them go.

CHAPTER TWO

WALKING WITHOUT A DESTINATION

For Gregory Pickett

It's easy to walk a lot of miles
When you don't have any place to go.

The walks close to home have sounds
As familiar as high school bands
Practicing, or a car radio, so loud
That crossing guards alert the troopers ahead.

Out of town walks have sounds
Unfamiliar (some soft – some loud).
Strange traffic patterns ahead,
Dim streetlights going on for miles,
And an anonymity which bands
The tourists together everywhere they go.

Alone, a walker could go five miles
In the city and not hear one loud
Scream or gunshot anyplace ahead;

The same walker in Iowa sounds
Fearless as he watches bikers go
Smoke in the parking lot with country bands.

With a partner, I can walk ten miles,
The words on her lips the only sounds
That matter in the next moments ahead;

We walk until hopelessly lost and go
Ask for directions from roving bands
Of teenagers, who don't even know they're loud.

It's easy to walk a lot of miles
When you don't have any place to go.

Nighttime forces you to study the bands
Of stars, until you find Polaris, ahead
Of the clouds carrying storms, loud
As cannons to the citizens startled by sounds.

Daylight brings its own problems, ahead
Of any other considerations; rock bands

Break up because the singer wants to go
Alone; the rest of us wander for miles,
Sing a bit off-key and a little too loud,
And fall in love with the way her name sounds.

I haven't a place where I really want to go,
And there's no place I would never go.
Walking without a destination is easier than it sounds.

SECOND SHIFT AT THE FERMILAB

We've set up picnic tables and chairs
In the old particle accelerator,
Contaminated the ion chamber
With cheeseburgers, soda, and chips,
Brought in a beach ball,
And encouraged the staff to strip,
Lose the lab coats and form a conga line.
The whole second shift dancing in our underwear,
ID badges swinging on the elastic
As a supervisor flips the switch.
Unhappy management helps insurrections succeed,
And we gauge our success,
By measuring the immeasurable,
Observing the unobservable
As paper plates and sexy lab assistants tumble inside
A two-mile tube at 70% the speed of light.

I am here and I am there.
Everything else is everywhere.
Uncertainty materializes as both particle and wave,
Like the moment a hot air balloon launches,
Like a conversation with a heretic,
Or how I imagine an identical twin
Would have turned out had she lived.
I stand in the middle of Fermilab,
A shop steward made of light
Part of a crazy collective,
A cobweb of colleagues, spinning,
Sparkling, time-traveling souls.
I just wanted to be part of an experiment,
Put in my hours from four to midnight,
Watch my young co-workers leave to meet at a pub
And never even realize that I just changed everything.

MY FIRST INCURABLE DISEASE

Certain pills I have to take make ghosts appear,
Lurking behind my back and visible only in mirrors.
I know they're just hallucinations
But they are better than the symptoms
Of my first incurable disease
Worthy of a second opinion.

I blame the insecticides sprayed on marijuana
Fields by the DEA, cruise ships docked
At oceanside bars, the way my uncle whistled,
And every Dionysian fantasy that got me
This disorder, now dramatized every night
In crazy-ass, surrealistic dreams.

I am waiting for my first hallucination
Inside of a dream, a surprise that violates
Verisimilitude, that questions the reality
Of the unreal like drawing a jack to fill an inside straight,
Or winning a hand with an ace and three wild cards
For the biggest pot of the night.

My favorite side effect, though, increases sexual desire.
These phantoms leave a little evidence behind:
An impression on a bedspread,
Perfume, red wine, jewelry discarded on a glass table,
Shapeshifting fingerprints, used ashtrays,
And a strip tease starting with the blouse.

Meanwhile, the second and third incurables
Subvert their very first cells
And start to affect the brain, the blood,
The nerves, the bones, and the tissues
Presenting the symptoms, while sparing the soul,
That imaginary me, outside the brain.

The soul's as real as you let it be.
It's the who that's always been there:
Flying, ephemeral, frightening
To the simple shepherds, still
Obsessed with the incurable, but immortal,
And that's all you can know when you're hallucinating.

MYSTICAL VISIONS AND COSMIC VIBRATIONS

I have spiked a pot of tea
With psilocybin, metaphors, and rum,
Dressed up in imaginary body armor,
Felt phantom raindrops on sunny days,

Watched sparrows graze the floors of outdoor cafes,
Sung schoolgirl songs in unpronounceable Vietnamese,
Lost myself in the scent of a dozen bouquets,
Saw the same visions; felt the same vibrations

That heavy-lidded hipsters, naked angels,
Cell phone rappers, Filipino girls, whose toes
Curl around their chairs, and a handsome young poet
Claim to have seen as a face reflected in water.

I stare so intently into the stillness of that lake,
Ripples form and a tempting goddess,
Peers right back up with hot green eyes,
Egyptian mascara, unblemished skin, and reproach.

I sit and sip my psychedelic tea.
Stars descend from above as the sound of raindrops
Falling off leaves in a breeze, hours after a storm.
They drip into puddles in a rhythm

Only a devoted disciple could comprehend.
I drink the night's starlight
Reflected in a freshwater stream
And glow like deer eyes in the headlights.

I am so high I never want to be sober.
I hear crickets, birds, the wind, the night, and the trees.
As if spinning, eyes shut, dizzy, tumbling over,
I savor as many minutes as I can seize.

STARLESS AT THE EQUATOR

For Matteo Perch Bigfish

Airfare to Quito's surprisingly cheap.
Thirty hours, though, including layovers,
But you know that. Your world has destiny.

Your family and friends live in the north.
They see dippers, Vega, and Cappella
Like any other stargazer in the hemisphere.

The southerners see crosses and pointers,
Clouds named for Magellan, starry galaxies,
Ancient worlds, now nothing but blurry dots of light.

You'll see none of that at the equator.
Clouds will sink inside the rain forest canopy.
Snowstorms will cover equatorial peaks,

The only snow not melting at that latitude,
And the sky will be a strange, empty template,
Its familiar stars straining at the poles.

It's your job to name new asteroids and comets,
Paint the slate with brand new constellations,
Make the newest collection of zodiac names.

You are the unnamed namer
As naked as Eve and Adam
Pointing, uttering, christening, full of joy.

You haven't even sinned yet;
You don't even need any dogma
To make the world real for those not yet born.

EASTER 2010

For Billy Tuggle

Your son looks just like Jesus.
Dark skin, white hair, short beard, great eyes
Like flames, sandaled feet burnished bronze

But with a flannel shirt and jeans
Thirty-one years old,
Two years before the big ministry.

He loves heavy metal music,
And instead of descending into Hell,
He takes a bus to metal bars on Saturday nights.

DUI. Suspended license. His father's car left home.
Wherever he eats is a banquet
As long as somebody else buys.

He uses flesh–colored earplugs
Like the bass player
He met the last time he was here.

He's been hassled by cops for crossing train tracks
While the warning lights and bell rang,
Just because he looked like that.

Still living at home and working sporadically,
He waits for the next two years
Of crowds, meditation, demons, and angels.

But today, Easter 2010 is a fresh April morning,
Empty but for unmarked cars, radar detectors,
Satellite photos, and a well–trained German shepherd.

Jesus is very much in demand on Easter.
Everybody wants to see him,

But he just wants to go to sleep
When he gets home at sunrise,
Because he stayed up so late last night.
So he sleeps – forever changed – paranoid –

Nerve-wracked – accused of harrowing hell.
Your son looks just like Jesus,
And he's why a new age must be born.

MY COUSIN'S CONSTRUCTION COMPANY

For Robert

We like to tear up the asphalt
On the city's expressways,
Put up orange wooden cones,
And let the holiday traffic
Honk for miles while we think
Of building new roads closer to home.
You and I take a Thanksgiving walk
In wool pants and brown shoes
From your mother's house
To the schoolyard on Augusta;

That's where as kids
We'd beg the pastor
To open the gymnasium
And let us shoot baskets
During the football games.
Now we are so stuffed
We need fresh air to belch,
And we're surprised when
Some kids' voices scream
When somebody opens the gym door.

It makes us walk
To the back of the parking lot
Beneath the Magikist Carpet Sign,
Big, red, neon-lipped billboard
That everyone used to describe
Our neighborhood to strangers.
Maybe it's the lights buzzing,
Or the rolling wheel drone
Of the road
Or the peppermint schnapps

We drank here as teenagers
That makes us try to climb
The billboard's rusty ladder.
Your foot in my hand,
Your hand grasping the cold
Metal bottom rung as you rise
Is nothing at all
When I hear you shout
That you can see the place
We should build our next road.

A CALL FOR MISSIONARIES

For John Shirk

Take to the sea in tall ships
And cross an ocean to get here.
We're the savages you need to save.

You won't find us in the jungle,
In mountainside caves, on the plains,
Or frozen in drifts of iglooed snow.

Your ministry's in the burlesque house,
Coffeeshop, tavern, and smoked-up two-flat
In the heart of Logan Square.

You preach to poets and actors,
Singers and comedians, magicians and artists,
With tattoos and rows of piercings.

You listen to the heresy, blasphemy,
Curses, pornography, and allusions,
Yet you hear the voice of Jesus as a whisper.

He calls to you while you are sleeping,
And enters your dreams disguised
As a soul you haven't thought about in years.

He traveled to India in his twenties,
Got a lot of strange ideas,
Brought them back home,

Caused a lot of trouble,
And wants you to do the same
For these heathens, smoking outside the bar.

See eternity
In the ink of a haiku.
Repeat until dazed.

See eternity
In the ink of a haiku.
Repeat until dazed.

The best missionaries succeed in saving themselves,
And creating a whirlpool in the river
The natives can't figure out how to avoid.

THAT SAME DREAM AGAIN

Buried in the fine print
      Of the credit card receipt
      She's been using as a bookmark,
Random letters shapeshift into

      Anagrams, code, and hidden messages.
She reads the rest of the disclaimer,
As if translated from Vedic scrolls
      As claims, warrants, and guarantees,

When the book falls on her lap.
      She sleeps like a contented cat.
      I envy her sound and quiet sleep,
Next to an open window, on a summer night,

      The kind I love, after storms have cooled the air.
She dreams she's a singer, solo on a stage
And puts her voice at the service
      Of the dark and silent audience

Like a scuba diver diving alone,
      In the cracked clamshell of a shipwreck.
      She dreams she's down there so deep
The tug of time slows everything down.

      She feels it as a current, the fish
Suspended at the edge of the weeds,
Fifty feet from today's unlucky lines and lures.
      She's in that same dream again,

The one she can't help but remember
      The one she can describe to a stranger
      But keeps secret from her family,
Husband, pastor, girlfriend, lover.

FALLING FOR THE MAGICIAN

He had me with the birds,
Flying in formation around his head,
And disappearing into a golden sack.

Poof! He tosses the empty bag
Into the audience and takes a bow –
Magician, hallucinogen, sorcerer.

It's his eyes, really.
Big billboard eyes hanging in a crowded lobby
Of a January lounge   filled with pickpockets and tricksters
                  shuffling among their tables and chairs.

Parking lot attendants trailing cold air behind them
When they come inside to take a break.

The candles shiver on our table,
The whisky glasses shake

The dried and brittle flowers in a vase
Stand ready to reanimate scented and luscious.

He's a blonde blue-eyed German and a dark
Brown-eyed Persian in a mirror holding a lamp.

I fall for him, the magician, at first sight,
And levitate myself onto his stage;
                  Cut me in two, suspend me on a pencil,
                  Sit in the air, the master of space,
                  Promise me anything, reveal nothing.

As he draws a Queen of Spades from every deck,
As he climbs a rope of scarves of many hues, colors, and tints
As he reads my mind and looks down my dress;
                  I spiral uncontrolled to his sighs, surprise,
                  deception, and lies

I long for his straight jacket escape,
But settle for him running through an
    alley in a cape.
See the show is over, and we're all out in
    the cold once again.

48

PLACES YOU USED TO WORK

For Christine K.

You've converted factories into lofts,
Grocery stores into chapels,
Airports into refugee camps;
You just can't forget places
Where you've toiled
And escaped to a better job.

When you set fire to a castle,
The flames leave a hollowed ruin
As big as a butte and haunted by spirits
From places we all have worked and left.
Ghosts of nurses and patients in a hospital.
Ghosts of waitresses and diners in a café.

They tug on your hair and shush you.
Appear just beneath the ivory tin ceiling
And just above the crocheted doilies
And teacup flowerpots you put on the tables.
The ghosts hang in the front window like lace curtains
Puffs of white make-believe erased from a blackboard menu.

You've got to start a company of one
Itinerant and impeachable, a laptop,
A cell phone, a P.O. Box, and a business card
With your name transcribed into braille.
You take meetings in hotel lobbies, libraries,
Museums, malls, gyms, bars, pubs, and the park.

You've even appeared on a college campus,
Or in other people's houses, till someday a parlor
Where you will teach us how to read tarot cards,
Notice our breathing, get comfortable in stillness,
Return to the ruins of places we used to work
And occupy every room like unbound souls.

WRITTEN IN TRANSIT

She adjusts her rearview mirror
To see the clouds
Above the row of cars behind her.

That view,
Which had been there all along,
Makes her think of other views
She had been too short or tall to see.

She dreams of things
The way she had as a girl.

Staring into the hot sky
Until she sees those figures
Made by the moisture in her eyes
Glide across her cornea
Like leaves and pads floating
Down a river at noon.

Then, we in the next car,
Silent and slumped in our seats,
Try to know just how she feels
Caught in airport traffic,

Listening to the horns
Of all the other drivers

Who want to wake us
From the dreams we have,
And the dreams of others
We can only guess about.

SMUGGLING IN GERMANS

For Pete Wolf

You asked me to smuggle a stone
Through customs for you;
I'm bringing in Germans instead.

I've packed them in my luggage
Along with the candy and liquor.
I've hidden a hipster waitress

A glassblower, two bakers,
And a couple named Heinrich and Gretchen,
Who have already taken a taxi downtown.

They've found a luxury suite
Where nobody knows them;
The street musicians counting coins

In front of the hotel,
The beggar next to the church,
The cop walking the beat.

Nobody sees them walk by.
I've smuggled them in flawlessly.
Their accents sound like church bells.

Their sweaters feel like blankets.
When you take their photograph,
Only the American buildings appear.

Heinrich, Gretchen, and the others,
Have memorized the local train lines
And exited at various stops.

You'll never find them now.
They're hiding in guest rooms
And spending only small bills.

They've unbundled their fragments
And infiltrated us.
You wanted a stone.
I'm bringing in Germans instead.

VILLANELLE IN A BOX

The fire always burns. Chicago glows gold and red. It's finally its turn. How much does it burn? Completely till it's dead. The fire always burns. It keeps its poets fed on flames they can't discern. It's finally its turn. Chicago learns to yearn. And refuses to take its meds. The fire always burns. A hundred years they said. Into a stony fossilized fern. It's finally its turn. And the rest of us learn to yearn. Wishing for the gold and red. The fire always burns. Until it is finally our turn.

TURNING INTO THE WIND

Chicago in the winter has calm days,
Sunny and mild, 32 degrees Fahrenheit,
Calm, the trees barely moving, yet noticeable.
The wind, when working windward, lets you zigzag
And get where you're going despite the chill.

The city is home to a school for alchemists:
Intro to Stones, Exploring Elixirs,
Just two of the courses in a comprehensive curriculum,
Including sailing and track for physical fitness,
Meteorology and Curses, possible electives.

There's going to be a call for gold, soon.
The school's recruiting and raising tuition.
Its ad campaign puts emerald tablets on posters
Hanging on the sides of buses and inside elevated trains
And challenges everybody to turn into the wind.

A few clever students figure it out, though.
They molt and shed and transform into breezes,
Reappear months later, southerly in springtime,
Straight from the west on the Fourth of July,
And they travel into the future,

As if waking from an induced sleep
Like an intruder in somebody else's dreams.
That's how they get there, knowing where
They've buried the gold, knowing it's worth
Ten times more than when they made it.

They get to live years longer than the norm.
Alchemists rarely retire. Why would they?
They hop through centuries ahead of the rest of us:
Epitaphs on stelae, ten-minute videotapes,
The best ones taken, when they don't know the camera's on.

REGARDING UTOPIA

They think they can build something perfect,
A castle on the tip of a peninsula
Separated from the mainland by a moat,
Where you leave all the doors unlocked,
Feed the neighbors, pray however you want,
And tolerate graffiti and revolution.

I spray paint footprints on the mailboxes
And stone walls, fight off their trances
And enchantment the way the west wind
Might breathe autumn into an August day
Scattering leaves on cobblestones,
Months before it's supposed to happen.

I love life in something, almost perfect,
Embrace quintessential sorrow
Savor lost loves and squandered fortunes,
Sunbathe half-naked next to the misty sea,
And protest perfection for the sake of stains,
Litter, diapers, stuttering, and white lies.

They have, in fact, created something perfect,
Perfect theatre, fiction, science, and art,
Reality projected on a movie screen,
A synthetic pearl, a silk rose,
A morning fog like an angel, a bodiless body
Who makes us forget everything one life to the next.

I am just trying to remember last night,
The utopian coffeehouses and pubs,
The latte, beer, vodka, and rum,
Taking a boat out into the bay
The illuminated castle like a chocolate candy
Ready for the continent to consume.

GIVING IT ALL AWAY

I got rid of it all.
Went bankrupt and foreclosed.
Donated all clothes and shoes,
And toys and ornaments.
Parked the car where it got towed,
Removed, the yellow numbers scrawled
In permanent marker on the back window.
I tossed a piano and stereo into a fire,
Traveled to a warmer climate,
And became a white shirt, trousers,
Sandals, and a satchel always empty.

I need nothing.
I walk up to my cuffs in the surf.
Dance without a conscience.
Own nothing but the scent of barbeque.
Have nothing but the lines I've memorized.
Sometimes I dream of the stuff I used to have.
It's submerged in water under a hole in the ice.
I descend into my cathedral of things.
Revel among my icicles and oyster shells,
Count phosphorescent jellyfish as my own,
And wake up relieved that I still have nothing.

I got rid of it all,
And now I have absolutely everything.
I have hours of time-lapsed weather
Clouds, sun, stars, and the moon.
I feel airwaves tremble like mandolin
And make willows dance with dreadlocks.
I listen to Spanish radio at red light crosswalks,
And I know the way your perfume travels
To the back when you enter a room.
All of those things that I am now able to own
I will give away again – and start over.

Mom in her rocking chair (Antigone)

Uncle Ray doing dishes

Eddie at the Door

Grandma's birthday 1957

New Year's Eve 1939

M.C. and his sister

Chicago snowstorm 1950

M.C. Rydel 1977

Bucktown before it became fashionable

M.C. Rydel 2022

A Tuscan Epithalamion

CHAPTER THREE

NEVER ULYSSES

I've always been a character actor;
Played sidekicks and henchmen.
Foreigners, sailors, go-betweens;
Gotten involved with spinsters;
Been made a fool of – by a vamp.

I have learned to concoct a glance
When the star changes his lines;
I've gone back to make-up, another hairstyle,
Maintained an inner flame with silence,
Remained loyal until it's my turn to die.

Is there a chance I will ever make it home?
Smell lush midsummer river willows?
Take tea, add sugar, eat shortbread?
Creak a painted Victorian porch swing
And listen for your Aeolian voice?

I am nothing but a soul who toils,
Sails west to new worlds by command,
Has fewer lines than ever, barely noticed;
Tell my son it is his turn to follow
To become a part of everything he sees.

ELEGY WRITTEN IN AN ICU

For Gene Gawalek

He was the soldier you didn't mess with.
Communists in Korea still fear him.
He spoke in declarative sentences, gifts
He could give like light on a rain-dimmed night.

Now the drizzle gives way to moonlight
Illuminating the hospital parking lot.
As heaven, with its saints in the heights,
Waits three days as we all occupy the ICU.

The hall's abuzz with youth and age:
Nieces, nephews, cousins, uncles, and aunts,
Eight in a room, breaking the rules, walkers, and canes
In defiance; he does in passing what authority can't.

He makes the ICU into his second acre,
Where shirtless on his tractor he cuts grass
Where at peace he plants a Japanese garden
Where meticulously he masters his craft:

Sundials, benches ceramic, a menagerie
Molded in concrete and cement, all in a line
Behind the ferns he planted last Spring
On a day after rain awash in sunshine.

He was the soldier you didn't mess with,
Who became husband, father, uncle, grandpa.
Immortal in memory, and where he now sits,
Next to God in glory atop the ramparts.

ELEGY FOR A MERCHANT MARINE

At his moment of death, everyone who loved him was in motion. His father captained another ship in the fleet. His mom in a taxi listening to Hindu music. Brothers and sisters in Mitsubishis and Audis. His girlfriend stepping slowly in line at airport security. His future love on the train from Mumbai to Jodhpur.

There, in the blue city, amid the crowds and painted buildings, where he would have met her had he lived, the world spins on its axis, the mariner falls to his death, and a militia boards his ship in the Strait of Hormuz.

His absence creates the world we know. And where he would have stood, eaten, drank, sat, and slept has been replaced by a where without him. The mariner never knew his death started a war, or that his Dad got promoted to Admiral. Mom elected to Congress. Mitsubishis and Audis the new Zeroes and Panzers. His girlfriend married to the Navy and a Commander.

And Jodhpur, the old city, the clock tower, the palace, the fort, eating Rajasthani food while the blue city sparkles below. And all, without the mariner. The love he'll never meet flies back to Riyadh. Her eyes so perfect, framed by a hijab, her smile so sudden, and she never even knew he existed. Her fate shaped by what never progressed.

THIRTY MORE DEAD IN AFGHANISTAN

August 2011

Regaining consciousness and sight,
I invoke the gods of chaos and light.
I watch fate-drenched mortals attack
In the name of demi-gods, monsters, intrigues, lies,
All for a love named Candy, who's as fragile
As chocolate, shaped like an hourglass.

I dance with Afghans at a campfire,
Make shadows like cave drawings on canyon walls,
Take hold of death, always just a coincidence away,
Just a dreadful click of a stray IED.

We dream of sleeping in tents with dark-skinned girls,
Soldiers themselves in the midst of their journeys,

Spread purple flowers all over a river,
Watch them congregate next to fallen trees,

Some find a current and go around
Like souls exchanging their here for there.

There is whatever paradise I can construct,
Hot as the Ganges in red silk and gold
Cold as speckled-salmon rivers north,
The water flows under the gates to the next life.

Yet, they are gone, and all of their plans are useless.
The little lies they needed day-to-day
Now lie interred with their bones.

Our memories of them feel like a breeze
A guest book makes when you flip the pages
Of ten thousand ink-pressed signatures.

And, like a sculpture's head lost to the sand,
The future is unfixable.
We fill every day's most quiet needs
Like lotus-eaters, embracing the sweet scent
Of forgetfulness.

WINDSWEPT AT THE DEMONSTRATION

Zuccotti Park, 2011

She's sweet disorder wrapped in a blanket.
Crimson hair thrown on her shoulders,
Dark eyes absorb the last light before sunset
As drums and voices and sirens and wind
Answer the cobblestone clomps of horses
Beneath the mounted police around our encampment.

They've let us keep the tents for one more night,
Let the library, soup line, medical staff remain
As November makes us seek cover
And cocoon in sleeping bags in the darkness.
She's willing to let me enter her dreams, she says,
Into the pathless woods of ghosts and crystals,

Premonitions and tarot cards, stars and beach fires,
Travelers and gypsies, pots of steaming soup, a waning moon,
And the buried streets of gaslights and hitching posts
That lie dozens of feet beneath this public park,
Once a maze of nineteenth-century avenues
That the city we occupy has built over.

She leads me out of this deep winter sleep
As the wind rattles our canvas walls
And the music finally subsides and the scents
Of makeshift dinners dissipate into the dew
Of tomorrow morning, when we march again
And mingle with the rest of the universe as an inconvenience.

THE NIGHT LIFE IN BABEL

Ever since the divine intervention,
The scene has expanded exponentially.
Animated Slavic, cell phone Chinese,
Whispered Farsi, and the only English
Belongs to a blind guy's screen reader
On his laptop with a synthetic voice.
This makes the nights in Babel important.
People stay awake just to hear
The old drinking songs in new languages.

Dogs, coyotes, and wolves have new howls.
The train whistles sound a little closer.
The Uptown wind sizzles in the bricks
Of the decaying ziggurats,
And the nightlife is all about body language.
Silk scarves; finger cymbals;
Bare midriffs; dangling cigarettes;
Soon everybody will stop talking
And listen to saxophones try to mix with cellos.

The memory of one language dissipates
Like the details of a dream at dawn.
The people wander among the ruins
Of their rubbled tower and along
Cobblestone paths to smoky dens.
They spend every night in a scattered city –
Some making myths. Some defying gods.
Some finding hope by trying to recall
Words they can no longer pronounce.

JOINING A CULT

This girl wants me to check out her cult,

Meet the congregation on Saturday night
Hear about the stuff they're giving up.

Giving up beer. Giving up breathing.
Giving up the flesh. Giving up all senses.

The old, losing vision, lose their car keys as well.
The deaf can't hear sounds that would scatter birds.

One old man reminds me of my dad,
Legs amputated, wheelchair arms.

A woman reminds me of my sister-in-law
Still smoking after a mastectomy.

The whole cult surrounds me
Like a room full of lit candles.

Apostles. Disciples. Missionaries.
Giving up the sensual for the divine.

I finally commit to a vow of silence.
I would give up everything to be with her.

MISTAKEN IDENTITY

I am always mistaken for someone else.
People walk up to me and call me names
Nowhere near my own.
I've been Bill, Bob, Ray, Eddie, Pete, and Swede.
Once a woman thought me her Senator
As he and I do, in fact, look alike,

But a Senator would not travel without
Three staff members, a security detail,
And maybe a reporter or two. Think it through.
Once, taking a shortcut through campus,
A Muslim woman in a hijab
Mistook me for her brother's academic advisor.

Another time, some little kid followed me
In line for a roller coaster ride
And held the hem of my jacket as if I were his father.
Last night, a stranger face-timed me by mistake
Thinking I looked like his cousin,
Insisting I still owed him something.

I spend my life looking like someone
Who looks like me.
Subway rides, coffeehouses, benches by the beach,
These settings present opportunities for confusion.
How can I avoid being in public?
I can't, and I really don't want to.

I've even been detained for eight hours in a small room
By customs agents at Chicago O'Hare
Because I looked like a Russian named Joseph,
I have been blamed, praised, lectured,
Loved, challenged, cajoled, dined, dated,
And married to people who mistake me for someone else.

People see the person they want to see in me.
Total strangers will eventually show up to my wake.
Two squads of gravediggers will meet at Plot 549.
The saints will make me wait a year in Limbo
Until they can verify exactly who I am,
And send my reincarnated soul to a completely different planet.

I am always mistaken for someone else.
Sometimes I carry my DNA sample
Just to make it through another day.
Even that does not convince the certain:
Certain that I am who they think I am
And not the person that I really want to be.

A CURE FOR AUGUST

We who know how to hide.
Take baths.

We turn off the lights,
Flip on the fan,

And slip beneath
Our ice cube masks.

I start thinking
Of thunderstorms

At our cottage up north,

All the uncles and cousins
Sit around a fan drinking beer,

Or summer with you
On the steps at night,

When we knew
All of our neighbors

And sang a cappella
With their kids

So light
I'd carry them home in pairs.

But I cannot bear to recall much more
Alone and cold in this dark tub,

So I rise shivering,
Noisy and older.

Grasp for air
And a cure for August.

ODE TO THE GIRL IN THE PHOTO

For Sara

She's as perfect as anyone you've never met.
Infallible, both young and old,
Light and dark, thin and soft,
Caught not posing in a candid shot
In the foreground of a black & white print.

She is looking at something out of the frame,
The world behind the photographer,
Its trees birds flowers
Nothing at all like the grey street and cars
Now captured, digitized, pixeled, and pinned to this wall.

She's for sale for over a hundred dollars
On consignment on a coffee shop wall,
Waiting for a marketing genius
To discover her, buy her rights,
Put her in an ad, just so she can sell perfume.

Geniuses seek the perfection she possesses
And obsess and desire and seek again.
They're not satisfied until her face
Fills every page 32 in every flight magazine
On every airliner flying above the globe.

Unattainable, untouched, air marshaled
She's bookmarked in the seatback in front of you.
Her perfume fills the first-class cabin.
A couple of passengers dream of her
As the plane begins its inevitable descent.

She's the girl in the black & white photo.
For sale on the coffeehouse wall.
Her soul, flawless, intact, everlasting,
Seeks to learn why it's getting any attention,
Seeks to learn if her body's been resurrected.

FABRIC OF COINCIDENCE

We are twins separated at birth,
One in Europe, the other in America.
We meet, sharing an Uber to the airport.
I get to hear my voice with an accent,
See my hair go gray in the temples,
Hear my ring tone play on his phone,
Learn that we live identical lives,
Experience irony the same way,
Say the same words at the same time.

We've exposed the fabric of coincidence.
Space and time like warp and weft
Guarded by three phantoms of fate.
The first specter spins the thread of life
From her distaff onto the spindle.
The second measures the thread with care.
The third cuts the thread as it unravels
With her abhorred shears and assures us
Of an identical demise on different continents.

Meanwhile, the fabric crackles
Like simultaneous signals in a circuit,
Which we monitor for car crashes, lotto numbers,
Telemarketers, robocalls, and left-handed signatures.
The fabric's all about passwords, captchas, and identical retinas
Who don't believe in either coincidence or fate.
Our twin faces neatly fit into the rearview mirror.
Our twin voices trail off like canyon echoes.
Our twin souls shine like young Cary Grants

Shirtless and lying in chaise longues;
Reading brown cloth first editions of *Anna Karenina*
Each wishing he'd been cast as Garbo's Vronsky.
One twin needs Gate A.
The other Gate Z for the non-stop home.
We have nothing left but an awkward...
Hug.

BLURRED EDGES

Professional photographers photoshop away
Every imperfection, erase a cowlick,
Hide the wrinkles, snip a jowl, touch up the eyes.
        What's left is magazine perfection,
        Which is no perfection at all.

Amateurs find beauty in subtle imperfection:
A cathedral's tilted rose window,
Spilt tea when the in-laws come over,
The moon obscured by treetops,
        And that deliberate flaw in a Persian rug,
        Because only Allah can achieve perfection.

I am no expert, barely competent with my phone;
Take photographs with blurred edges,
Unintentionally,   Ring a bell at midnight,
        Burn incense in hallucinogenic tents,
        Sleep like a tonsured monk on a donkey
        Leading astray everyone else in the dream.

Dreams have a special imperfection.
The backup singers are a little off-key.
Cities in the clouds sway in the wind.
        People who you've known your whole life,
        People you've seen only once on a subway
        Follow you like a procession of sins.

You've discovered a way to take photos
Inside your dreams and sell them for a profit.
        What makes them authentic are the blemishes,
        Nine and a half by eleven paper,
        Foie gras and baguettes with the wrong wine,
        Erotic books, secret looks, and anything forbidden.

I buy your photos when I'm in them,
Just another character with flawed beauty
                Withered and lean, aging with grace,
                Broken seashells on a Florida beach.

NEW YEAR'S EVE IN PARADISE

Time sweeps her hand across the Earth
Like a monstrous spirit, the size of suns,
Who brushes invisible moments onto all of us
As her gleaming lamplit gaze dazzles like starlight.

She rattles the earthen-floor tin shacks
Of our island without monsoon flash
Or trade wind blast – and shimmies westward
Sprinkling joy and sorrow on the faces of clocks,

Wrapping moments of tawdry lace
Into glinting, clinking, noisy British glass,
Seeping through overcast cracks like a melting moon
Illuminating Bronze Age hunters on the hills and reaves.

I can see her blue snowstorms creep on radar screens
And make their way across the frozen lake,
Muffling music in Michigan huts
With the smell of whiskey on her breath.

She won't make it to Hawaii for hours,
Until then, here I wait in Paradise, thirty-eight minutes,
Counting, forgetting, distracted and drinking,
Knowing it is time to change my life.

SEDUCING A WIDOW

For Zach

Move at least a thousand miles away,
Especially when you are young and still stumbling
Into discoveries of unestablished significance:
Brazilian orchids that may cure asthma;
Lightyear-long radio waves, incomprehensible;
Sauces of garlic, ginger, mango, and butter.
Then, you just have to let it go,
Like a water skier dropping the ropes
Or a litterer with cellophane, or like a widower yourself,
Just letting everything go, as he unwinds,
Unties, unfastens, and loosens his first widow
Who has been convinced, to let everything go.

Make yourself a thousand years old.
Live twenty lives. Remember them all.
Tell stories. Listen to the wind. Take naps.
Soon, you will be all alone, a cynic in the subway,
Homeless, living in a barrel, writing messages
All over dollar bills, defacing people's money
With obscenities, ideas, and ransom notes.
That is what will get her attention.
Make her see you for as young as you are.
Muscles in gym shorts, a day-old beard,
Hairy arms tuning an acoustic guitar
As you wait for her to come to you in her bed.

Move another thousand miles away.
Disappear like a sports car passing on the right,
Linger like a piano pedal's last long note,
Find a beach, a sunset, a skyline,
Forget everybody, look for something new,
Spend time with tender piercings and tattoos.
She will decide to move a thousand miles too,
Maybe more, looking for untrodden villages,

The French coast, lights gleaming and then gone,
Until she shows up years later as a postcard,
A single line of text in code, read aloud,
Nothing but syllables and ink, languished, forlorn, and bereft.

82

THE BALLAD OF THE PURLOINED JOURNAL

She wrote her name on the inside cover
Dotting every "I" with a little star,
And she drew tattoos in her worn diary
As I stared from the back of the railway car.

She sat alone from the suburbs to the city,
Read a book, closed her eyes, lightly snored.
The conductor collecting tickets woke her
And inhaled the perfume in her every word.

The train was a midday local
Bringing the second shift workers downtown.
They exhaled the darkness scattered around her.
She stood out like an onyx star on a crown.

Her face had an appealing sadness
Like a Venetian blind unrolled;
Dark skin, black clothes, dyed hair,
Sparkling jewelry, eyes like coal. A future foretold.

She made another sketch in her journal
Captioned the picture with ink-black verse.
Suddenly turned her head in my direction,
Caught me in my hunger and my thirst.

The car jostled, shrieked, and came to a stop.
She buttoned her jacket and wrapped a scarf on her face.
The train emptied quickly without me.
She had left her diary in its place.

I took it and searched for her on the platform,
Got a sinister look from a transit cop.
Now I fight off the temptation to read her pages
And wait daily for her to reappear at every stop.

THE QUOTIDIAN

It's a beast who hypnotizes me
Every day of my life
Like a cat skipping
Over a black telephone
Six or seven times in a row.

Its muted clawless paws
Landing on the glass tabletop
As I wait for your phone call
And fast forward last week's
Television shows and wait.

I'm days behind everyone else
And feeling inside-out.
My nerves like shirt seams
On top of my skin,
The scent of grass

The moist air,
And the train whistle
Drifting into our room
With the Summer breeze
And the hum of the ceiling fan.

I like to leap completely
Out of myself
The way joy bounds out
Of the neck muscles
Of a violinist as he plays.

Flying above
The room I'm part of,
I am a parabola of yellow light
Curving out of the bottom
Of its lampshade to the floor.

While the rest of me
Shines upward,
A duplicate curve of light
Yellow and smoky
Glaring on the wall.

Outside the Summer sky
Its stars and sheer clouds
On a night without moonlight
Reminds me how endless space is
How the only way we cross it

Is to die and reincarnate
Ourselves out there.
Our city's a pattern
Of artificial light.
Here and there the beacons

Of vacant lot fires
Spark when somebody breaks
Bottles of booze in them.
Church bells and headlights
Go off during communion

Of the Saturday night masses
Scattered around town.
The beasts prowl the alleys.
Their cat eyes like headlights
Shine on the fire escapes

That some of us use
When we land.
The quotidian has me hypnotized
As subtle as baking scents
Make me wish you were here.

When the telephone rings
Beneath the springing cat,
Who shrieks and kicks the lamp cord
I scramble in the darkness
To get to the phone before you give up.

LOVE POEM POSTED ON THE INTERNET

I have been seeing you everywhere,
Turning left on an arrow in traffic,
Training for a marathon around a tiny, windy lake,
Taking tea at a sidewalk café.
Those brown eyes and hair and white skin
Are as fresh as after a shower
And as white as your terrycloth towel
As you dry your wet hair and disrobe.
The white shoulders, breasts, stomach, and thighs
Become everything all morning into the night.

I make room for your triumphant return
By abandoning all grudges and blame.
I forgive all lost luggage and the baggage handlers who lost it.
All lost reservations and frazzled clerks
All thieves, cheaters, liars, and frauds.
I am as empty as a newly built cabin
And as cluttered as a sublet in Greenwich Village.
You have been spotted by the paparazzi,
All eyelashes, bobbed hair, and smile,
And you make wherever you are into a stage.

You have become a character in a poem
Written by a character in a poem.
You exist in the "About Us" section of your theatre's website,
In safety deposit box photographs,
In person at an airport during a weather delay,
And you want us to be young lovers again,
Who notice no one around them when they kiss,
Who stretch and yawn as they wake at noon,
Who hear phantoms in a windswept window,
And who search the net for poems posted like beacons.

LIVING AS A TURK IN ÇANAKKALE

You tell me about your life.
I tell you about mine.
We cross the Dardanelles
And lease a room in Çanakkale.

The time before I met you
Flickers like images on a cineplex screen,
Like a pattern of nerves; like a sidewalk
Windblown with red pine needles.

Nothing existed before you.
Young lovers create words,
Which when we're much older
Seem meaningless to their new loves.

Construction workers eat their lunches
Next to the traffic gridlock they cause
On the road between our room and the ferry,
Taking tourists to the ruins of Troy.

Rubbing out the mark your ring makes,
You warn me French women have no problem
Expressing discontent and criticism, and have
No hesitation in asking for what they want.

Well, now you want me to be a Turk,
Frame myself in a huge crescent moon,
Big and yellow, learn how to seduce,
How to help you desire.

The night settles into a windless stillness.
Music, so foreign, is everywhere.
We roll back our eyes and peer upward
And live for one day in Çanakkale.

CHAPTER FOUR

OUR COLLECTION OF MASKS

We were ready for the pandemic.
Survived it by wearing masks.

Thousands of masks.
Some for performance.
Some for protection.
Some for disguise or ritual.
Some for theatre and others for masquerade.

Masks of sequined gold, ivory, and silver,
Pairs of black Roman masks.
A whole rhinestone, ram horn, antlered room of masks.

The smallest, painted oyster shells,
Finger masks used for storytelling and dancing.
The largest, a giant totem, covers the whole body.

A goalie mask and a police riot mask
From our Chicago two-flat,
The fencing and ski mask
From our apartment in Grenoble,

Two masks from Cameroon,
An impala and a lion,
Communicate with spirits living
In forests and open savannas.

A married couple in Siberia walks
Bareheaded along a frozen lake
Until their faces turned as red as masks
Chiseled in a block of shining ice.

All of these masks
Kept the virus out of our lungs,

So twenty years later, kids born today
Can wear their favorite masks tilted,
So other survivors can again feel the danger
Of their unmasked faces.

SONG FOR A NURSE

I saw you on the Channel 2 evening news,
Waving to other nurses ending a 12-hour shift.
A taxi out front. A masked runner in view.
You offer your time to others as a gift.

The pandemic has shut down the city.
A single-engine plane in the night sky.
Your corporal works of mercy done without pity.
Old souls leave old bodies when they die.

The gold coast shops are boarded with plywood.
Cafes abandoned. Drug stores – down to one line.
You don't charge for medicine, though you could,
Until the last door you reach begins its chime.

Still masked and gloved, you walk alone
Through neighborhoods empty and silent.
Your home sits in the city's demilitarized zone,
Bordering on the most violent.

You're the nurse going door to door.
Have you heard you were on the news?
You came off as noble, honored, adored,
As a nurse with no choice but to refuse.

IN MEMORY OF GREGORY CURRY

He died about a week before the virus
Locked all of us into our homes for months,
Waiting for his funeral postponed.

As if capsized, shipwrecked, marooned,
Surviving on crabs and coconuts,
We dared not step into the street.

The city outside could just as well be the sea:
Underwater playgrounds with no kids,
Discarded papers, wrappers in the current,
Apartments with their shades pulled,
Bouquets blooming for no one,
The few castaways left, avoiding each other's breath.

Into this deep, we must commit Curry's body.
His sartorial presence tailored and pressed,
A cape, a cap, and calabash pipe,
A room at the Plaza, seven hundred a night.
What skeleton Capote will host his masked ball?
What coral-tinged seabed will welcome him?

We don't want him washing up like Shelley,
So we take him at least four nautical miles out.

If we're lucky he'll fall into an old shipwreck
Where his soul knows a doorway,
Passes through a doorframe's missing bottom,
And finds the route to Elysium beneath a broken mast.

The sea receives its honored guest.
The colder, the deeper, the better, the best.
Curry haunts beaches — now off-limits to all.

He boards schooners silently like a stowaway.
The cargo hides him like a dressing screen.
He waits to emerge on Judgement Day,
"When the sea shall give up her dead."

THE OPPOSITE OF AN ELEGY

For Daniel McNeil

How can I write an elegy for someone who cannot die?
Who survives a plague hidden like a hostage?
Who cannot establish proof of life;
Whose name goes adrift in a breeze on a ransom note.

You're the silence before chamber music begins,
Before the violin, cello, and viola play a first note.

You feel more like a presence than an absence.
Like the sound of bedsheets on a clothesline,
Or the surf, a birdsong, a ticking clock, or muffled conversations.

I keep traces of you in my phone as voicemail
And as the confetti you sent in a text message
For my birthday, the last tacit evidence of you.

You live in the recordings you once played for me,
In the blood moving chamber to chamber
Until it's loaded like a gun some judge keeps
In his chambers before rendering an opinion;

I have such a hard time writing about you,
Until I hear you in the drumming of a djembe.

Your soul seeps green through my runcible spoon,
Pours itself into the glass of emerald absinthe
I taste as the anise of my grief.

Command this line of poetry to resurrect you,
To cajole a description of oblivion out of you,
To hear of twisted vines and nightshade in the afterlife.

You have become nothing but a turned stone,
Spilt spices, wordless expressions, a missing face,
And the silence of a Sikh,

Calm since he knows nothing ever dies.
Still, I take our morning walk without you,
Frozen, windswept, sunlit, abandoned,
My silver coins a ransom the kidnappers,
As invisible as an airborne virus, covet.

I dare you to prove everybody wrong,
Spring out of cold chaos fully grown
And live forever as the end of this song.

DRIVE-BY DAYDREAMS

For Cesar

My cop friend writes sonnets in his squad car
During his lunch break, mastering rhyme and meter,
Caesura and volta, metaphor and couplet,
As he eats the bologna and cheese on a Kaiser roll
His wife and son made for him at breakfast,
Or so the daydream goes.

He says he needs these daydreams
As much as he needs to stay alert,
For drive-by shootings on the west side:
Attempted murder, robbery and battery,
Aggravated assault, ending in a car chase,
With the unlawful use of a weapon – all on his shift.

He says he needs these daydreams
As much as he needs his vest and badge,
As teenagers gather in Garfield Park,
As the cars under the Lake Street L tracks
Wear slats of sunlight punctuating a shadow,
Or so the daydream goes.

He says he needs these daydreams
As much as he needs his partner riding
In his blue and white, his red and black district
The one that gets the drive-by shootings,
Where you can catch a stray bullet in the head
While sitting on your sofa in the living room.

He says he needs these daydreams
As much as he needs a night of thunderstorms,
As a guy in a wheelchair selling snow cones gets shot
Not far from a friend's Chicago bungalow, where his son
Plays in the yard, with the scent of grass, tulips, barbeque,
Or so the daydream goes.

He says he needs these daydreams
As much as he needs the clouds and the wind,
Trees and lightning bugs, sparrows in his birdbath,
Or toddlers who drop their cherry ice cream,
As their mothers grieve their older brothers,
And just can't look at him, or any other cop, anymore.

My cop friend finishes his sonnet at the station,
Rhymes breast, unrest, breath, and death
Drives home on a street beneath red light cameras.
Tonight chicken, corn, biscuits, wife, and son,
A new moon at perigee, huge in the sky.
Or so the daydream goes.

HOT BATH IN WINTER

I could drink brandy all night
While the steaming beige water drains,
Or I can press my fingers
On my larynx
To clear the nasal taste
From my throat,
But I'd rather submerge myself
And watch steam rise from me
Like an apparition.

It will come visit me
When I'm sixty-five
Voiceless and cold after a stroke.
I will be sitting in a car
Frosted by my breath
When it appears.
Snow will gather on the edge
Of the windshield like the soap
On the surface of this water.

Starting up the car,
I will watch the exhaust
Burn a drain into the street ice.
Behind me, again submerged,
I will recognize the apparition,
My younger self.
Reaching to it, my arms will be bandages
Joining our chests together
Pressing the two sets of lungs
Forcing the air
To break the clot within our throats
Making each man speak.

WHITE IN THE MOON MY YOUNGER SELF APPEARS

For A.E.

It's dangerous for old men like me to walk
And circumnavigate a subdivision alone.
Families are sheltered inside.
Their dogs lie still at their children's feet.
The fog gently lifts. April trees bud.
White in the moon my younger self appears.

Twenty-five and fearless, he's writing a poem
With too many allusions, searching for the divine
Like someone new to the Kabbalah.
The scent of fireplaces, the wind in the trees,
Gutters rattle, one airplane in the sky, we hike.
Both men, apparitions to the other, now body and blood.

He asks – What did I do before I became you?
Abandon home for dorm for studio for bungalow.
Confession, wedding, baptism, holy orders.
The brown hair grey – the brown beard greyer,
We're doppelgangers on the shores of Lake Zurich
Without a soul outside, without a thought within.

What can I do to never become you?
Keep splitting infinitives. Separate yourself
From the rest of the procession. Embrace young envy.
Rekindle old lust. Ditch the deadly others.
Let the wind swirl in the dust.
And ascend on a cloudless night into the past.

Leaving me here, he must have listened to what I said.
My house is dark and empty. In the driveway, no cars.
The garage door code no longer works.
I can charge thousands on my credit cards,

But I can't find an open hotel.
There's no place where anybody wants me.
We who know how to survive
Learn to live by staying inside.
Millions will die. The old must hide.
The street breathes danger that's hard to resist.
This pandemic may last for years, when
White in the moon my younger self reappears.

UNDER HOUSE ARREST

My family and friends are all confined to their homes.
They're stuck wearing monitored ankle bracelets
And fear signaling the cops downtown.
My sister is mixing an elixir that turns blood to gold;
A dear brother-in-law listens to public radio alone.
The kids aloft on high-rise balconies with city views.
Grandma bakes. Aunts and Uncles dance.
My cousin the actor works on his lines.
All of us lonely. All of us confined.

The judge had it in for us, I say.
I shouldn't have whistled and hooted
When the wedding party passed by.
I shouldn't have covered up the scent
Of the opium den in my car
With the smoke of a Cuban cigar.
I should have bribed security,
Coerced the inspector, found a merciful Magistrate,
But it all went bad, so here I am.

Go ahead, let me dress up in a tuxedo.
Tell my wife that we'll spend visiting hours in the hall.
Tall and stunning, blonde in a red wine dress.
She makes quite an entrance.
The champagne takes the sting out of the occupation
As we dance all night to *In the Mood.*
A few celebrities leave in roadsters or sedans.
Everyone else is scheduled for a midnight video
Most are in the shower or fixing their hair.

I'm in the house for the next year and a half.
The shingles rattle on the twenty-year roof.
The window seals between the panes are broken.
A clanging, gurgling noisy sump pump.
The flowers and bushes in bloom.
The backboard is loose. The driveway's cracked.
Segregated, secluded, separated, sequestered,
I quarantine by order of an invisible warden
My blood turns gold yet I go to bed still under house arrest.

A FEAST DURING THE PLAGUE
– A SONG

> Now the church deserted stands
> School is locked and dark.
> Overgrown are all our lands
> Empty groves are stark.
> Now the village bare as bone
> Seems an empty shell;
> All is still – the graves alone
> Thrive and toll the bell.
> > Pushkin, 1830

I defy death by inviting you all
To a feast at my place near the park.
The play's been canceled, the theatre closed,
The actors make their way here before dark.

Together, we fill our plates with rationed cheeses;
Serve duck, salmon, beer, and wine;
Dish out pastries, ice cream, cakes and cobbler;
Pour the liquor. Break the law. Risk a fine.

Everyone invited made it, still in costume,
Though the theatres have long been closed.
Vagabonds and outcasts, knights and princes,
It's hard to keep them quiet or composed.

I dance too close to a row of torches
Mounted in my waterfront cave near Galilee.
What a time to begin a public ministry
In a land of gloom in a time of mortality.

I move my consciousness from one plane to the next.
Feel time as a torrent through willows and birch.
The party ends with one last drinking song when
We hear the bell of a distant church.

Everyone leaves one by one, the police
Follow a few disciples on the one-way streets.
The curfew begins just after midnight.
They walk home as the sheltered city sleeps.

I defied death by inviting you all
To a feast at my place near the park.
The play's been canceled, the theatre closed,
The actors make their way home in the dark.

THREE SECONDS WITHOUT DR. JOHN

Admitted to some hospital as a patient,
The Doctor's irregular heartbeat is seen
As routine for the emergency room.
Stop his heart. Let it start itself again.
Let the pain rattle around a lobe in his brain.
Send him back home. A doctor.
John is glad he's not in his hospital.
The story of palpitations while running,
How he's in the ER during a pandemic
Instead of delivering Spring babies,
How they took him to the ICU
Where they saved him intravenously.

It would be around his hospital
Like a virus – like a rumor – ever-mutating.
The dose of adenosine, like a spike
Deep into the Achilles tendon,
Pierces his heart with a momentary death –
Three seconds without Dr. John.

Rip the soul right out of his chest
And let it see what it cannot have,
A square in Paris where lovers sip
Wine and eat, where a parrot,
Green with hints of red and blue, sits in a window
And watches the pedestrian parade.

His soul sees what most of us picture, what Paris
Ought to look like. The cobblestone streets.
A bistro. A small grocery store. Artists. Motorcycles.
Green vines climbing to a blue roof.
Montmartre. A taxi to the hill in the 18th arrondissement.
Dark-eyed boys and girls staring at each other.
No one sees Dr. John.
He's gone as quickly as he came.
The half-life of adenosine is ten seconds.
The discharge papers already printed.
His wife orchestrates his release. The wheelchair's there.
She takes him back home where it's safe.

HOME REMEDIES

Great Grandma traveled before the pandemic
To the foothills of the Tatra mountains,
Only to shelter for weeks in her cousin's cabin.
Her grandmother had cured the flu with garlic,
Used vinegar for bruises, and cabbage for ulcers,
The same way, for centuries, grandmothers used to do.

None of it works on this virus.
No more than holy water, or candles, or prayers;
No more than a relic, talisman, or amulet,
Can stop curses, charms, and magic.
None of them brings the fever down.
They're better at undoing spells.

Great Grandma walks in secret all night,
Past a garden, fruit trees, and a steeple.
She hears wolves and brown bears growl,
Watches comets reflect in a shimmering lake,
Waits for her cousin among the fingered boat slips
Idling in gear, making no wake.

Pale, weary, companionless,
Predictable as the phases of the moon,
She waxes and wanes, new and full,
Repeating the same story each day
About a special moss grown in a cave
The key to her cousin's discovery.

They are close to a cure,
Let others seek vaccines and treatments.
Mix the magic moss with oil and vinegar
And crumple the butt of a smoked cigar into a jar.
Buried for weeks, it congeals into a paste
Applied on the neck till the fever breaks.

The virus detaches. The lungs heal.
They take their miracle international.
The airports break all the rules,
Send a private jet to retrieve them.
As the world waits for the next pandemic.
Their home remedy makes them stars.

ONE WAY TO KRAKÓW

I have packed a dozen rooftops in my bags,
Lakeside cottages loud with cicadas,
An open library window near Harvard Yard,
Voyeur high rises across from hotels,
Scented gardens in Midtown Manhattan,
All packed in luggage chosen just for this trip.

I fly first class to Warsaw
Three thousand dollars American.
Layover for two hours for an hour flight to Kraków
To an apartment hosted by Anna
On Miodova Street near the Jewish Square,
Where from this rooftop I can see the river.

I've become obsessed with rooftops.
Church spires, red shingles,
Outdoor lookouts attached to the castle
The market, bicycles, spiraling roads
Around a green and verdant mound
A museum with an ancestor enshrined.

Anna, how I've become obsessed with you.
Teach me the language.
Let me hang out with your friends.
Dinner after a movie with no subtitles.
I slice the vegetables. You make the soup.
My week is more than half done.

The sun sets late here in June.
The light fades on a painting of Chopin.
I've seen mermaids white-haired in the sea.
The week concludes; we have a last cup of tea.
One last chance to plummet from this roof.
A coward. I'm gone before I know the truth.

YOU'RE ALREADY IN HEAVEN

You're already in Heaven.
It's just not that good.
You've won fifty dollars
In a million-dollar lottery,
Used all your buy-one-get-one-free coupons,
Found a case of beer
Hidden from the cops by kids,
Discovered Paradise in cloudy days and ice,
And have fallen in love with tussled hair,
Aches, complaints, and a burning soul aglow.

In a previous life,
You always rode the subway alone
Nearly every midnight, every Friday.
Your last life was filled with passengers
Who exited at previous stops;
They have become the life you miss
Like the water in a dried-up well,
A building torn down years before,
A bridge overrun by a flood.
You long for what's no longer there.

Now in this life,
It's always unlucky October, cold blue clouds,
Dark brown leaves, standing water,
And Divinity hiding underground
Like a dandelion root clutching the dirt and waking.
In Heaven, you still have free will.
You can choose to fight the angels,
Get tossed off a crystal wall,
From morn to noon still fall,
And end up right back here, no place at all.
You're already in Heaven.
It's just not that good.

ACKNOWLEDGMENTS

"A Call for Missionaries" *CC&D Magazine.* Vol. 282 April 2018. Online Journal.

"A Feast During a Plague – a song". *Balcony Magazine.* Vol 2 Number 2. Page 23.

"An Elegy to Uncle Ray" *Lucky Star.* Volume 2 Number 1 October 1984. Page 48.

"Bat Hunting" *Shadowboxing.* Volume 5 Number 5 November 1987. Page 7.

"Blurred Edges" *Batayan.* Volume 14, 2019. Page 67.

"Eclipse" *The Oyez Review.* Number 13 Spring 1985. Page 67.

"Fabric of Coincidence" *Batayan.* Volume 15, 2019 Page 9.

"Falling for the Magician" *Batayan.* Volume 7, 2018. Page 65.

"Giving It All Away" *Twisted Vine Literary Arts Journal* Number 4 Spring 2015. Page 102.

"Home Remedies" *Batayan.* Volume 20, 2020. Page 12.

"In Memory of Gregory Curry" *Batayan.* Volume 20, 2020. Page 12.

"Letter to Antigone" *Chanterelle's Notebook.* Volume 34 Summer 2014. Online Journal.

"Love Poem Posted on the Internet" *Batayan.* Volume 5, 2016. Page 31.

"Mistaken Identity" *Down in the Dirt Magazine.* Volume 155 March 2018 Online Journal.

"Months of Immortality" *Caravel Literary Arts Journal* Volume 1 Fall 2015. Online Journal.

"My Lebanese Friend" *Down in the Dirt Magazine.* Volume 155 March 2018 Online Journal.

"New Year's Eve in Paradise" *Batayan.* Volume 16, 2019. Page 13.

"Placebo Effect." *Batayan.* Volume 18 2019. Page 5.

"Regarding Utopia" *Down in the Dirt Magazine.* Volume 155 March 2018. Online Journal.

"Second Shift at Fermilab" *CC&D Magazine* Vol. 282 April 2018.

"Seducing a Widow" *Caravel Literary Arts Journal* Volume 1 Fall 2015. Online Journal.

"The Day We Learned to Read Palms" *The Oyez Review.* Number 13 Spring 1985. Page 68.

"The Quotidian" *Shadowboxing.* Volume 5 Number 5 November 1987. Page 6.

"Thirty More Dead in Afghanistan" *Down in the Dirt Magazine.* Volume 126 December 2014. Online Journal.

"Three Seconds without Dr. John" *CC&D Magazine* Vol. 311 July 2021.

"Turning into the Wind" *Down in the Dirt Magazine.* Volume 125 November 2014. Online Journal.

"Under House Arrest" *CC&D Magazine* Vol. 310 June 2021.

"Walking without a Destination" *Caravel Literary Arts Journal* Volume 1 Fall 2015. Online Journal.

"White in the moon my younger self appears" *Down in the Dirt Magazine.* Volume 176 October 2020. Online Journal.

"Windswept at the Demonstration" *Caravel Literary Arts Journal* Volume 1 Fall 2015. Online Journal.

SPECIAL THANKS TO LITERARY JOURNALS AND THE *IN ONE EAR* OPEN MICROPHONE VENUES

Thank you to Jill Charles, Janet Kuyper, and Eric Allen Yankee for bringing many of these poems to an audience from their editorial offices in Chicago, Illinois, Austin, Texas, and Perth, Australia. I would also like to say "thank you" to Pete Wolf, Sara King Winninger, and Billy Tuggle for running the *In One Ear* Open Mic for over 30 years, most recently at Flatts and Sharpe Music on Sheridan Road in Rogers Park, Chicago.

ABOUT ATMOSPHERE PRESS

Atmosphere Press is an independent, full-service publisher for excellent books in all genres and for all audiences. Learn more about what we do at atmospherepress.com.

We encourage you to check out some of Atmosphere's latest releases, which are available at Amazon.com and via order from your local bookstore:

Until the Kingdom Comes, poetry by Jeanne Lutz

Warcrimes, poetry by GOODW.Y.N

The Freedom of Lavenders, poetry by August Reynolds

Convalesce, poetry by Enne Zale

Poems for the Bee Charmer (And Other Familiar Ghosts), poetry by Jordan Lentz

Serial Love: When Happily Ever After… Isn't, poetry by Kathy Kay

Flowers That Die, poetry by Gideon Halpin

Through The Soul Into Life, poetry by Shoushan B

Embrace The Passion In A Lover's Dream, poetry by Paul Turay

Reflections in the Time of Trumpius Maximus, poetry by Mark Fishbein

Drifters, poetry by Stuart Silverman

As a Patient Thinks about the Desert, poetry by Rick Anthony Furtak

Winter Solstice, poetry by Diana Howard

Blindfolds, Bruises, and Break-Ups, poetry by Jen Schneider

Songs of Snow and Silence, poetry by Jen Emery

INHABITANT, poetry by Charles Crittenden

Godless Grace, poetry by Michael Terence O'Brien

March of the Mindless, poetry by Thomas Walrod

In the Village That Is Not Burning Down, poetry by Travis Nathan Brown

Mud Ajar, poetry by Hiram Larew

To Let Myself Go, poetry by Kimberly Olivera Lainez

ABOUT THE AUTHOR

M.C. Rydel lives in his native city of Chicago, worked for years as a Dean for the Hadley Institute for the Blind and Visually Impaired, and now teaches literature and creative writing at Loyola University Chicago. M.C. has published poems in a variety of journals and performed them at such iconic venues as Heirloom Books, Wicker Mic, the Elevator Sessions, In One Ear at the Heartland Café, and Flatts & Sharpe Music Company in Chicago, and the Parkside Lounge in New York City.